Recipes from Around the World

$\mathcal{F}$AVOURITE POTATO DISHES

IMP Limited

CONTENTS

$\mathscr{P}$OTATOES — THE PICK OF THE CROP

Whether baked, boiled, mashed, sautéed, chipped or roasted, potatoes are always popular. Here's how to identify and make the most of the different varieties.

FRIED OR BOILED?

Some potatoes are great for mashing, others are better baked, chipped or boiled. It all depends on their texture.

Floury potatoes break up easily when cooked. These types of potato are excellent baked, mashed or roasted. King Edward, Pentland Squire and Golden Wonder are popular varieties.

Waxy potatoes hold their shape well during cooking and have a firm, yet tender, texture. They are ideal for boiling and sautéing, for chips and for salads. Varieties include Cara, Estima, Pink Fir Apple, Nadine and Marfona.

All-purpose potatoes perform well whether you mash, chip, boil, bake or roast them. Desirée, Maris Piper and Romano are good all-purpose potatoes.

Choose potatoes that are well-shaped, clean and firm to the touch. They should be free from any cuts and blemishes.

Store potatoes in a cool, dark airy place, preferably in a paper sack with the top folded over. Do not keep them in plastic bags as they can trap moisture and spoil the potatoes. Most types of potato should be used within 1–2 weeks, but new potatoes only last about 2–3 days, so buy them in smaller quantities as required.

TASTY POTATO TIPS

• Dice **waxy potatoes**, parboil, then sauté in olive oil with black pepper and finely chopped sun-dried tomatoes.

• Line a greased flan dish with mashed **floury potatoes**; fill with beaten eggs, diced ham, crème fraîche, cooked peas and seasoning. Bake at 180°C/350°F/Gas 4 for 15 minutes, or until golden.

• Parboil **waxy potatoes**, then grate and mix with a little Cajun seasoning. Form into cakes and fry in groundnut oil.

• Toss **new potatoes** in prepared pesto sauce for an easy side dish.

• Slice baked **floury potatoes** in half and top with passata, sliced mozzarella and pepperoni. Grill for 5 minutes, or until golden.

- Liven up mashed **floury potatoes** by mixing in some grated Cheddar cheese and a little Dijon mustard just before serving.
- Toss roasted **all-purpose potatoes** with chopped fresh parsley and grated Parmesan.
- In summer, wrap cooked **new potatoes** in foil with red pesto sauce and grated cheese. Cook on a hot barbecue for 10–15 minutes until the potatoes are hot.
- Top baked **floury potatoes** with butter mixed with grated lemon rind and chopped dill.

NEW POTATOES

New potatoes are the first crop of potatoes available each year. To test for freshness, hold one between your thumb and first finger and scratch the skin — it should just flake away. Do not store them for too long or they will lose their wonderful, earthy flavour. There is no need to peel them, just scrub or scrape clean before cooking. Varieties include Epicure, Nicola and Jersey Royal.

METHOD	VARIETIES		TIP
BAKING	Cara, Desirée, Estima, Saxon Golden Wonder, Marfona, Maris Piper	CARA	Rub some oil and salt into the skin before baking to make it crisp
BOILING	Cara, Cosmo, Estima, Jersey Royal, Marfona, Nadine, Rocket, Saxon	ESTIMA	Keep the cooking water, which is high in nutrients, for making soup
CHIPPING	Cara, Desirée, King Edward, Maris Peer, Pentland Dell, Saxon	SAXON	Fry chips in small batches in hot oil to ensure they cook evenly
MASHING	Desirée, King Edward, Maris Piper, Pentland Dell, Romano, Wilja	KING EDWARD	Mix in a little warm milk to the mash for a really fluffy texture
ROASTING	Desirée, King Edward, Maris Piper, Nadine, Romano, Sante, Wilja	DESIREE	Roughen the outsides before roasting for a crispy finish
SALADS	Anya, Desirée, Jersey Royal, Maris Bard, Pink Fir Apple	BABY JERSEY ROYALS	Add lemon juice to the cooking water to preserve colour

ENGLISH PARSLEY POTATOES

GREAT BRITAIN

Parsley and potatoes are perfect partners. Here, the potato slices are coated in a rich and creamy sauce that is flecked with green to make a simple, yet stylish, dish.

INGREDIENTS
(Serves 4)

- 800g/1¾lb all-purpose potatoes, e.g. Maris Piper
- salt and black pepper
- large bunch of parsley
- 1 onion
- 15g/½oz butter
- 2 tbsp plain flour
- 125ml/4fl oz vegetable stock
- 125ml/4fl oz milk
- 250ml/9fl oz double cream
- 1 tbsp Worcestershire sauce
- 1 egg yolk

INGREDIENTS TIP

Flat-leaved parsley is more aromatic than the curly-leaf variety but either is suitable for this dish. It is worth chopping a large quantity in a food processor, then freezing it. Use straight from frozen, within three months.

1 Peel and wash the potatoes and cut them into medium-thick slices. Put into a pan of cold, salted water, cover and bring to the boil. Reduce the heat and simmer for 10 minutes, or until just tender.

Step 1

2 Wash, dry and finely chop the parsley, discarding the stalks. Peel and chop the onion. Melt the butter in a large saucepan and fry the onion until transparent. Stir in the flour and cook, stirring, for about 1 minute. Mix together the stock, milk and cream and pour into the pan, stirring continuously. Whisk until the sauce boils.

3 Drain the potatoes in a colander, then mix into the cream sauce. Add half the chopped parsley and season with salt and pepper. Add the Worcestershire sauce.

Step 2

4 Simmer the potatoes gently in the sauce for 10 minutes until tender, stirring occasionally. Lightly whisk the egg yolk with most of the remaining parsley, then stir carefully but thoroughly into the potato mixture. Cook for a further minute, without allowing the sauce to boil. Serve sprinkled with the remaining parsley.

Step 4

Preparation **10** Min Cooking **25** Min
Per Serving: 545 kcal/2272 kJ;
8g protein; 35g fat; 52g carbohydrate

TYPICALLY ENGLISH

Worcestershire sauce has been made to a secret recipe, based on vinegar, molasses, sugar, anchovies, tamarind, garlic, shallots and spices, for more than 150 years. The sauce adds piquancy to sauces, stews and traditional dishes such as Cottage Pie.

COOKING TIP

The potatoes in this dish are in a creamy white sauce, thickened with a paste of butter and flour, known as a roux. The paste is cooked for 2-3 minutes to prevent the sauce having a floury taste. To ensure that the sauce is smooth, pour in the liquids gradually and whisk continuously until the sauce boils.

SERVING TIP

The perfect accompaniment to roast beef, served with English mustard and peas.

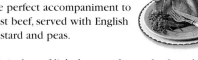

 A glass of light beer, such as pale ale or lager, would go well with this dish.

COLCANNON MASHED POTATOES

IRELAND

Delicious Colcannon is an ever-popular Irish dish of mashed potatoes with colourful Savoy cabbage and tasty spring onions. It makes a comforting winter warmer.

INGREDIENTS

(Serves 4)

- 800g/1¾lb floury potatoes, e.g. King Edward
- salt and black pepper
- 250g/9oz young Savoy cabbage
- bunch of spring onions
- 50g/2oz butter
- 250ml/9fl oz milk
- pinch of grated nutmeg
- 2 tbsp chopped parsley, to garnish

INGREDIENTS TIP

The light flavour of young Savoy cabbage is best in this dish but any variety of round, fairly loose-leafed cabbage can be used. However, avoid older cabbages with large tough leaves.

1 Peel and roughly chop the potatoes, then cook them in lightly salted, boiling water for about 15 minutes, or until just tender when pierced with the point of a knife.

2 Meanwhile, discard any tough or damaged outer leaves from the cabbage. Wash the inner leaves and discard the core from each leaf. Finely shred the leaves.

Step 2

3 Bring a large saucepan of salted water to the boil and cook the cabbage, covered, for 5 minutes, or until tender. Drain thoroughly in a colander. Wash, trim and thinly slice the spring onions.

4 Melt the butter in a pan and cook the spring onions for 2 minutes. Stir in the cabbage, then pour in the milk. Bring to the boil, then immediately remove from the heat.

Step 4

5 Drain the potatoes in a colander, then return them to the pan, or place in a large bowl, and mash until smooth. Stir the cabbage mixture into the potatoes and season with salt, pepper and nutmeg. Sprinkle with chopped parsley before serving.

Step 5

Preparation **10** Min Cooking **25** Min
Per Serving: 306 kcal/1288 kJ;
8g protein; 11g fat; 46g carbohydrate

TYPICALLY IRISH

The potato, at one time the staple diet of the Irish, has been both a blessing and a curse. Despite crop failures that brought severe famine to the country, potatoes still feature in many typical Irish dishes, such as fried potato cakes and potato and parsley soup.

COOKING TIP

To chop parsley quickly and easily, put a few sprigs into a mug or measuring jug and cut with scissors until finely chopped. This method also works well with other herbs, such as chives, coriander and dill.

SERVING TIP

Colcannon mash is good with grilled sausages or bacon, or with cooked meats, such as ham and salami.

 A glass of stout, such as Guinness, makes a satisfying and fitting accompaniment.

9

$\mathscr{S}$MOKED SALMON SALAD

SWEDEN

A light, creamy dill mayonnaise enhances the flavours in this delicious salad of tender potatoes, lightly cooked mange tout and delicate strips of smoked salmon.

INGREDIENTS
(Serves 4)

- 600g/1lb 5oz new or waxy potatoes, e.g. Jersey Royal or Pink Fir Apple
- salt and black pepper
- 100g/4oz mange tout
- 100g/4oz gravad lax or smoked salmon
- 4 tbsp mayonnaise
- 6 tbsp single cream
- 1 tbsp lemon juice
- 3 tbsp chopped fresh dill, plus dill sprigs to garnish

INGREDIENTS TIP

Gravad lax is a Scandinavian delicacy of salmon marinated for several days in coarse salt and dill. It has a subtle flavour. There are many types of ready-made mayonnaise available from supermarkets. Choose a good-quality one with a mild, creamy flavour.

1 Scrub the new potatoes or peel older waxy potatoes. Cut large older potatoes across in half. Cook the potatoes in lightly salted, boiling water until tender. Allow 10–15 minutes for small new potatoes or 20 minutes for large older potatoes.

2 Meanwhile, wash the mange tout and trim the tops and tails. Add to a small saucepan of salted boiling water, cover and cook for 2–3 minutes, or until just tender but still with a slight crunch. Drain in a colander and rinse under cold running water.

3 Drain the potatoes and allow to cool slightly, then slice them fairly thinly. Cut the gravad lax or smoked salmon into thin strips with a sharp knife.

4 In a bowl, mix the mayonnaise with the cream, then add the lemon juice. Stir in the chopped dill and mix well.

5 Arrange the potato slices, mange tout and salmon on four plates. Spoon the mayonnaise and cream dressing over each salad, allowing it to trickle between the potato slices. Garnish with dill sprigs and season with freshly ground black pepper.

Step 2

Step 3

Step 4

Preparation **10** Min Cooking **25** Min
Per Serving: 333 kcal/1399 kJ;
11g protein; 17g fat; 37g carbohydrate

TYPICALLY SWEDISH

Gravad lax literally means buried salmon, because it was originally stored for times of need. After a good catch, Swedish fishermen would bury casks of the salmon deep in the ground. Today gravad lax is a famous speciality, available all year round.

COOKING TIP
The ingredients for this smoked salmon salad can be prepared several hours in advance, but be sure to store them in separate, airtight containers in the fridge. Assemble the salad on individual plates just before serving, to retain the separate flavour and texture of each ingredient.

SERVING TIP
Serve this dish as a starter, or for a light lunch with apple cake and custard for dessert.

Serve with aquavit — a Swedish spirit flavoured with caraway seeds — or a chilled beer.

SERVING TIP Offer the canapés with drinks or serve them with rye bread as a starter.

 Serve with Danish beer and chilled schnapps, a fiery spirit distilled from barley and potatoes.

DANISH POTATO CANAPES

DENMARK

Slices of potato make an excellent base for these rich fish morsels. Dill-flavoured crème fraîche and a sprinkling of red lumpfish roe add a touch of class to each canapé.

INGREDIENTS
(Serves 4)

- 6 long waxy potatoes, e.g. Belle de Fontenay or Pink Fir Apple
- salt and white pepper
- 90ml/3fl oz crème fraîche
- 2 tbsp mayonnaise
- 2 tbsp fresh dill
- 1-2 tsp lemon juice
- 50g/2oz smoked salmon
- 60g/2½oz each kipper and smoked mackerel fillets
- 2 tbsp red lumpfish roe

TO GARNISH
- lettuce leaves
- small fresh dill sprigs

INGREDIENTS TIP

Red or black lumpfish roe makes an attractive, and much more economical, alternative to real caviar which comes from the sturgeon fish. Orange salmon roe could also be used.

1 Scrub the potatoes under cold running water and cook in lightly salted, boiling water for 20 minutes, or until tender. Drain, leave to cool slightly, then peel and cut into 2cm/¾in thick slices. Discard the rounded ends of the potatoes.

Step 1

2 In a small bowl mix the crème fraîche, mayonnaise and dill, then add salt, pepper and lemon juice to taste.

3 Cut the smoked salmon into bite-sized pieces with a sharp knife. Remove the skin from the kipper and mackerel fillets by holding the tail end and pulling the skin away from the flesh. Cut into bite-sized pieces.

Step 3

4 Top each slice of potato with one or two slices of either kipper or mackerel, or a twist of salmon. Finish with a spoonful of dill cream and a little lumpfish roe.

5 Wash the lettuce leaves individually under cold running water and pat dry. Arrange them attractively half way around the edge of a large serving plate. Place the canapés on the plate and garnish with dill.

Step 4

Preparation **20** Min Cooking **20** Min
Per Serving: 326 kcal/1366 kJ;
16g protein; 14g fat; 35g carbohydrate

TYPICALLY DANISH
The Danish island of Bornholm in the Baltic Sea is renowned for its hot-smoked herrings, known as bornholmers. During the summer, the smokehouses operate non-stop as the fish are hung over smouldering wood chips to give them their distinctive flavour.

HASSELBACKS

DENMARK

These sliced potatoes, baked to crisp perfection in the oven and flavoured with different tempting seasonings, were invented by Mrs Hasselback as a speedy alternative to baked potatoes.

INGREDIENTS

(Serves 4)

- 12 all-purpose potatoes, e.g. Romano
- salt and pepper

FOR THE HERB MIXTURE

- 50g/2oz butter
- 2 tbsp chopped fresh parsley or 2 tsp dried
- 1 tbsp chopped fresh oregano or 1 tsp dried
- 1 tbsp chopped fresh basil or 1 tsp dried

FOR THE CHILLI MIXTURE

- 1 tbsp vegetable oil
- 1 tsp paprika
- 1 small red chilli
- 1 tsp chopped fresh coriander

FOR THE GARLIC MIXTURE

- 2 cloves garlic
- ½ lemon
- 1 tsp chopped fresh rosemary
- 1 tbsp olive oil

1 Scrub the potatoes and pat them dry, then cut a thin slice off one side of each to form a flat base. Slice each potato thinly, taking care not to cut right through to the base. Carefully open up the slices and season well with salt and pepper. Preheat the oven to 170°C/325°F/Gas 3.

Step 1

2 For the herb mixture, melt the butter in a small pan and stir in the herbs. Spoon over four of the potatoes.

3 For the chilli mixture, mix together the oil and paprika. Spoon over four more potatoes. Wash, de-seed and chop the chilli. Mix with the coriander and sprinkle between the slices. Wash your hands well.

Step 3

4 For the garlic mixture, peel and finely chop the garlic. Wash the lemon, grate the rind and squeeze the juice. Mix the rind with the garlic and rosemary. Pour the olive oil and lemon juice over the remaining four potatoes. Sprinkle the garlic mixture between the slices.

Step 4

5 Place the potatoes on a greased baking tray. Bake in the oven for about 50 minutes, or until crisp and cooked through.

Preparation **50** Min Cooking **50** Min
Per Serving: 268 kcal/1566 kJ;
10g protein; 4g fat; 79g carbohydrate

TYPICALLY DANISH

Fish is a very popular ingredient on Danish menus, especially lightly salted herrings known as matjes. Salmon is another favourite, along with eels, oysters and cod. Danes will drive miles to visit an inn that is reputed to serve the best eels.

COOKING TIP
When cutting the potatoes into slices in Step 1, use two wooden spoons to prevent the knife slicing all the way through. Hold the spoon handles securely on either side of the potato, then cut down as far as the spoons will allow. Make sure the slices are fairly thin and even so that the potatoes cook through.

SERVING TIP
Serve with grilled salmon and a mixed pepper, green bean, sweetcorn and tomato salad.

 Sparkling apple juice or cider makes a refreshing drink with these Danish potatoes.

POTATO PANCAKES WITH APPLE SAUCE

GERMANY

Fried to perfection, these pancakes are golden and crisp on the outside and moist on the inside. The spiced apple sauce makes an excellent sweet and sour accompaniment.

INGREDIENTS

(Serves 4)

FOR THE APPLE SAUCE

- 575g/1¼lb tart eating apples
- 3 tbsp lemon juice
- 1 cinnamon stick
- 200ml/7fl oz dry cider or unsweetened apple juice
- 2 tbsp sugar

FOR THE PANCAKES

- 800g/1¾lb floury potatoes, e.g. King Edward
- 1 onion
- 3 eggs
- 75g/3oz sour cream
- 60g/2½oz fresh white breadcrumbs
- salt and black pepper
- sunflower oil, for frying

INGREDIENTS TIP

For a tasty sauce use tart, juicy eating apples such as Jonagold or Cox's Orange Pippin.

1 For the sauce, quarter, core and peel the apples, then slice finely. Put into a saucepan with the lemon juice, cinnamon stick, cider or apple juice and sugar. Bring to the boil, reduce the heat and simmer for 20 minutes, stirring occasionally, until very soft. Leave to cool. Preheat the oven to 110°C/225°F/Gas ¼.

Step 1

2 To make the pancakes, peel and wash the potatoes. Grate them by hand or use a food processor. Squeeze out any excess moisture by pressing the grated potatoes in a folded clean tea towel, then put in a bowl.

3 Peel and finely chop the onion. Lightly beat the eggs. Add to the potatoes together with the sour cream and breadcrumbs. Season, and mix thoroughly.

Step 2

4 Heat a little oil in a large frying pan. For each pancake, place about 2 tablespoons of potato mixture into the pan and flatten with a fish slice. Fry the pancakes in batches, until golden brown underneath, then carefully turn and cook until golden on the other side. Keep each batch warm in the oven until all the pancakes are cooked. Serve immediately with the apple sauce.

Step 4

Preparation **25** Min Cooking **20** Min
Per Serving: 439 kcal/1848 kJ;
11g protein; 13g fat; 65g carbohydrate

TYPICALLY GERMAN

In Germany, reibekuchen, or potato pancakes, have long been one of the most popular everyday dishes. They are often served as a sweet treat or snack, sprinkled with caster sugar or served with a fruit compôte and sour cream.

COOKING TIP

To make really crispy pancakes, cook in a non-stick frying pan coated with a thin layer of oil. Do not turn over the pancakes before the edges are brown and crisp. When they are cooked on both sides, drain on a sheet of kitchen paper to soak up any excess fat and stop the pancakes turning soggy.

SERVING TIP

These pancakes are delicious for lunch, with kebabs or grilled sausages and bacon.

 Serve with a glass of dry cider or, for children, apple juice with lemonade.

SERVING TIP Serve with lightly cooked carrots tossed in butter and chopped fresh tarragon.

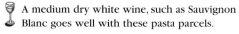 A medium dry white wine, such as Sauvignon Blanc goes well with these pasta parcels.

CHEESE AND POTATO RAVIOLI

AUSTRIA

Tender pasta pockets conceal a creamy potato filling flavoured with chopped fresh herbs. A speciality of Carinthia, this dish is served garnished with crispy bacon and herbs.

INGREDIENTS
(Serves 4)

- 275g/10oz plain flour, plus extra for dusting
- 4 eggs
- salt and black pepper
- 150g/5oz floury potatoes, e.g. King Edward
- 2 tbsp sour cream
- 250g/9oz cream cheese
- 3 tbsp chopped fresh herbs, such as chervil, parsley, chives and mint
- pinch of ground nutmeg
- 1 rasher rindless streaky bacon, to garnish
- 25g/1oz butter
- chopped fresh chives, to garnish

INGREDIENTS TIP

Either use one particular herb to flavour the filling or mix the four suggested herbs, using slightly less mint than chervil, chives and parsley.

1 Mix the flour, 3 eggs, a pinch of salt and about 5 tablespoons water to make a firm dough. Wet your hands and knead the dough into a large ball, then leave to rest in a covered bowl for 30 minutes.

2 Meanwhile, peel and wash the potatoes. Cut them into chunks and cook in salted, boiling water for 15 minutes, or until tender. Drain and return to the pan or place in a bowl. Mash until smooth. Mix in the sour cream, cream cheese, chopped herbs and nutmeg. Season with salt and pepper.

3 On a lightly floured surface, roll out the dough until about 3mm/⅛in thick. Cut out about twenty 7.5cm/3in circles. Beat the remaining egg. Brush the edges of the dough circles with beaten egg and put 1 teaspoon of potato filling in the centre of each. Fold the dough over and press the edges to seal.

4 Bring a large pan of salted water to the boil, add the ravioli and simmer for 10 minutes until cooked. Chop the bacon. Melt the butter in a frying pan, add the bacon and fry until crisp. Drain the pasta and serve topped with the bacon and chives.

Step 2

Step 3

Step 4

Preparation **30** Min Cooking **25** Min
Per Serving: 668 kcal/2785 kJ;
16g protein; 45g fat; 52g carbohydrate

TYPICALLY AUSTRIAN

Carinthia, Austria's southernmost region, is directly influenced by its neighbour, Italy, and is renowned for its pasta. The lush, green pastures are ideal grazing land for cattle and their rich milk is perfect for making topfen, a soft cheese used as a ravioli filling.

ℬACON ROSTI

SWITZERLAND

Waxy potatoes are grated and fried to make rösti — a classic Swiss savoury pancake that is crisp and golden outside, yet meltingly soft within. Streaky bacon makes it extra tasty.

INGREDIENTS

(Serves 4)

- 750g/1lb 10oz waxy potatoes, e.g. Cara
- salt and white pepper
- 75g/3oz rindless streaky bacon
- 5 tbsp vegetable or sunflower oil

INGREDIENTS TIP

It is now possible to buy different styles of bacon that vary according to their curing method. Dry cure bacon is best for this recipe as it produces very little liquid when fried. Use smoked or unsmoked according to personal preference.

1 Peel and wash the potatoes, then cook them in lightly salted, boiling water for about 20 minutes, or until tender, but still firm. Drain, and leave to cool for 15 minutes.

2 When cool enough to handle, coarsely grate the potatoes by hand or use a food processor. Put in a bowl and season with salt and pepper. Finely chop the bacon.

Step 2

3 Heat about half the oil in a large frying pan to coat it thinly, and fry the bacon until crisp. Add the grated potato and spread out evenly over the base of the pan, using a metal slice or spatula. Press down into a neat cake.

Step 3

4 Fry the rösti over a low heat for 10–15 minutes, or until the underside is golden. Do not lift the edges until it is well cooked or the rösti may fall apart. Drizzle the remaining oil over the top.

Step 5

5 Take the pan off the heat. Loosen the rösti around the edges and slide it onto a plate. Put another plate on top, turn the rösti over, then remove the top plate. Carefully slide the rösti back into the pan and fry for a further 8–10 minutes, or until golden brown underneath. Serve immediately.

Preparation **30** Min Cooking **40** Min
Per Serving: 424 kcal/1768 kJ;
7g protein; 26g fat; 42g carbohydrate

TYPICALLY SWISS

Swiss cooking is known both for its excellence and diversity, which includes influences from Italy, France, Austria and Germany. Rösti is now popular worldwide, along with native Swiss cured meats and rich fondue cheeses such as Gruyère.

COOKING TIPS

As the potatoes need to be cold before being grated, rösti is the perfect dish for using up leftover boiled potatoes. Store them in the fridge overnight in a covered container • Waxy potatoes are the best for rösti as they have a rich, golden colour and provide a good texture when grated.

SERVING TIP

Serve rösti with a mixed green salad for brunch or with a vegetable casserole for a light lunch or supper.

Serve with a dry white wine, such as Chardonnay, or a spritzer of white wine with mineral water.

DUCHESSE POTATOES

NORTHERN FRANCE

INGREDIENTS
(Serves 4)

- 500g/1lb 2oz floury potatoes, e.g. King Edward
- salt and white pepper
- 2 egg yolks
- 4 tbsp single cream
- vegetable oil, for greasing

INGREDIENTS TIP
Peppercorns freshly ground in a mill have the best flavour but ready-ground is an acceptable alternative. White pepper is used to season this recipe as black will leave dark flecks and spoil the appearance of the creamy, pale potato swirls.

Transform plain mashed potatoes into a sophisticated dinner party dish. Beneath the crisp, browned outer crust is an interior that is deliciously creamy.

1 Preheat the oven to 200°C/400°F/Gas 6. Peel and wash the potatoes, then cut into thick slices. Place in a saucepan, add cold water to cover and a little salt. Bring to the boil, reduce the heat and simmer for about 15 minutes, or until tender.

Step 2

2 Drain the potatoes and purée to a fine pulp with a hand-held electric whisk or fine masher. Beat the egg yolks with the cream, then add three-quarters to the potatoes and beat in. Season. Set aside the remaining egg mixture for glazing.

Step 2

3 Grease a baking sheet with a little oil. Spoon the potatoes into a piping bag fitted with a large star-shaped nozzle.

4 Pipe swirls of potato slightly apart on the baking sheet. Be sure to pipe a solid base and centre, so no pockets of air are left in the middle.

Step 4

5 Carefully brush the swirls with the reserved egg and cream glaze. Bake in the oven for about 20 minutes, until golden brown. Remove from the baking sheet with a metal slice and serve immediately.

Preparation **30** Min Cooking **35** Min
Per Serving: 208 kcal/871 kJ;
5g protein; 9g fat; 28g carbohydrate

TYPICALLY FRENCH
The 1890s were known as la belle epoque in Paris when colourful personalities of the day, such as the Prince of Wales patronized the city's chic restaurants. One popular place was Maxim's which was famous then, and remains so today, for its elegantly presented dishes.

COOKING TIPS

The potatoes are baked in a hot oven so that their surface browns quickly and the swirly shapes are not lost • The potato can be piped onto trays lined with cling film and frozen until solid, then packed in freezer bags. When ready to serve, cook from frozen in a 180°C/350°F/Gas 4 oven for 20-25 minutes.

SERVING TIP

Duchesse potatoes are a stylish accompaniment to any roast joint, or to grilled salmon steaks.

Choose a dry white wine, such as Sancerre or Pouilly Fumé.

CROQUETTES WITH CHEESE

NORTHERN FRANCE

Light, mashed potato surrounds a creamy centre of melted cheese and is coated with crisp golden breadcrumbs, making a delicious alternative to plain potato croquettes.

INGREDIENTS
(Serves 4)

- 500g/1lb 2oz floury potatoes, e.g. King Edward
- salt and black pepper
- pinch of grated nutmeg
- 3 tbsp chopped fresh parsley
- 2 egg yolks
- 2 tbsp plain flour, plus extra for dusting
- 150g/5oz Port Salut cheese
- 1 egg
- 50g/2oz dried breadcrumbs
- 50g/2oz Parmesan cheese
- sunflower oil, for deep-frying

INGREDIENTS TIP

Port Salut cheese has a soft texture and mild flavour. It is named after the abbey where it was first made by Trappist monks. You can use Edam or Saint Paulin cheese instead.

1 Scrub the potatoes and cook them in lightly salted, boiling water for about 20 minutes, or until tender. Drain and leave until cool enough to handle. Peel and mash.

2 Season with salt, pepper and nutmeg. Add the parsley. Mix in the egg yolks and flour to form a stiff dough.

Step 2

3 Slice and discard the rind from the Port Salut and cut the cheese into sticks. With floured hands, take a plum-sized portion of the potato mixture and shape it into an oblong roll. Press a piece of cheese into the centre and press the potato round it. Re-roll the potato to make the croquette shape.

Step 4

4 Break the egg into a shallow dish and beat with a fork. Put the breadcrumbs into a second dish. Grate the Parmesan and mix with the breadcrumbs. Using two forks, roll the croquettes in the beaten egg, then coat them with the breadcrumb mixture.

5 Heat the oil to 180°C/350°F, or until a cube of bread turns golden in 30 seconds. Fry the croquettes in batches for 5–10 minutes or until golden. Remove with a slotted spoon, drain on kitchen paper and serve.

Step 5

Preparation **20** Min Cooking **35** Min
Per Serving: 473 kcal/1972 kJ;
18g protein; 30g fat; 34g carbohydrate

TYPICALLY FRENCH

Restaurants on Mont-St-Michel, an island just off Normandy, offer dishes made with local produce, such as 'Sole à la Normande' (sole poached in cream) and 'Tarte Normande de Lisieux' (apple tart). Calvados (apple brandy) and Camembert are also local specialities.

COOKING TIP

If you have time, put the shaped croquettes onto a plate at the end of Step 3, cover with cling film and chill in the fridge for an hour or longer. This will help firm up the mixture so that the croquettes will keep their shape better when coated in the egg and breadcrumbs as well as during frying.

SERVING TIP

Serve the croquettes with grilled steak and mixed salad drizzled with an oil and vinegar dressing.

🍷 This dish will be complemented by a fruity French red wine such as a Corbières or Fitou.

SERVING TIP Accompany the gnocchi with crusty bread for a sustaining supper.

Serve with a full-bodied Piedmontese red wine, such as Barbaresco, or Barolo.

POTATO GNOCCHI

NORTHERN ITALY

These small, light potato dumplings, known as gnocchi, are extremely popular in northern Italy. They are delicious with a tomato sauce, fresh sage leaves and a sprinkling of Parmesan.

INGREDIENTS
(Serves 4)

- 1kg/2¼lb floury potatoes, e.g. King Edward
- salt and white pepper
- 800g/1¾lb ripe plum tomatoes
- 2 small onions
- 15g/½oz butter
- 16-20 small fresh sage leaves
- 200-250g/7-9oz plain flour, plus extra for dusting
- 50g/2oz Parmesan cheese

INGREDIENTS TIP

Plum tomatoes have a fuller flavour than other varieties. They are excellent for making a sauce, particularly when they are ripened in the sun. If they are out of season, use two 400g/14oz cans of tomatoes, and a few finely chopped sun-dried tomatoes. Add to the onions in step 2.

1 Peel the potatoes and cut in half. Cook in salted, boiling water for 20 minutes, or until tender. Slit the tomato skins with a sharp knife. Place the tomatoes in a bowl, pour over boiling water and leave to stand for 1 minute. Drain and remove the skins. Cut in half, de-seed and chop coarsely.

2 Peel and finely chop the onions. Melt the butter in a saucepan and briefly fry the sage leaves, then set them aside. Fry the onions in the butter until transparent, then add the tomatoes. Season, then simmer, uncovered, over a low heat for about 20 minutes.

3 Drain and mash the potatoes, then season. Using a spoon and then your hands mix in the flour a little at a time to make a stiff dough. Dust your hands with flour and shape the dough into 2–3cm/¾–1¼in long rolls. Roll them on a fork to mark ridges.

4 Cook the gnocchi in batches in a large saucepan of salted simmering water for 5 minutes, or until they float. When cooked, remove with a slotted spoon and keep warm. Pour the tomato sauce over. Garnish with the fried sage leaves. Grate over the Parmesan and serve immediately.

Step 2

Step 3

Step 4

Preparation **40** Min Cooking **20** Min
Per Serving: 444 kcal/1883 kJ;
14g protein; 7g fat; 86g carbohydrate

TYPICALLY ITALIAN

Gnocchi originated in Piedmont, but are popular throughout northern Italy. They are served at major celebrations such as New Year's Eve or on carnival Friday when, in Verona, gnocchi are offered to anybody who passes the basilica San Zeno Maggiore.

3 WAYS WITH MASHED POTATOES

Mashed potatoes take on a variety of styles around the world.
Serve these alternatives for a tasty change.

HERBY MASHED POTATOES

Preparation **10** Min   Cooking **20** Min

GREAT BRITAIN

(SERVES 4)
- 1kg/2¼lb floury potatoes, e.g. King Edward
- salt and black pepper
- 125ml/4fl oz milk
- 50g/2oz butter
- 90ml/3fl oz single cream
- 1 tbsp chopped fresh parsley
- 2 tbsp snipped fresh chives

1 Peel the potatoes and cut into quarters, or eighths if large. Cook in salted boiling water for 20 minutes, or until tender. Drain; return to the pan.

2 Bring the milk to the boil in a separate pan. Gradually pour it over the cooked potatoes and add the butter, allowing it to melt.

3 Beat the potatoes with a hand-held electric whisk until they reach a smooth and creamy consistency.

4 Heat the cream in a small saucepan without allowing it to boil. Lightly beat the cream into the potatoes with some salt and pepper. Mix the herbs together and sprinkle over each serving of potato.

TWO-COLOUR

Preparation **10** Min

CARIBBEAN

(SERVES 4–6)
- 400g/14oz floury potatoes, e.g. King Edward
- salt
- 400g/14oz sweet potatoes
- 25g/1oz butter
- 125ml/4fl oz single cream
- 4 tbsp milk
- 1 tsp ground allspice

1 Peel the potatoes and cut into large pieces. Cook in salted boiling water for 20 minutes, or until tender.

MASH

Cooking **20** Min

2 Meanwhile, peel the sweet potatoes and cut into quarters, or eighths if large. Cook in salted boiling water for 20 minutes, or until tender.

3 Drain the potatoes and mash with half the butter and the single cream to form a creamy, smooth consistency. Drain the sweet potatoes and return to the pan. Add the milk and the remaining butter, then mash. Stir in the allspice.

4 Add the sweet potato mash to the plain mash and swirl the mixtures together with a spoon to create a marbled effect. Serve immediately.

HEAVEN AND EARTH

Preparation **20** Min   Cooking **35** Min

GERMANY

(SERVES 4)

- 1kg/2¼lb all-purpose potatoes, e.g. Maris Piper
- salt and black pepper
- 2 large onions
- 100g/4oz rindless streaky bacon
- 50g/2oz butter
- paprika, to garnish

1 Peel the potatoes, cut into large pieces and cook in salted boiling water for 20 minutes, or until tender.

2 Peel and thinly slice the onions. Chop the bacon.

3 Melt half the butter in a frying pan and fry the bacon until crisp. Remove with a slotted spoon and set aside. Add the onions to the pan and cook gently, stirring occasionally, for 5 minutes, or until soft.

4 Drain the potatoes and return to the pan. Add the remaining butter and season with salt and pepper, then mash. Stir in half the onions and half the bacon.

5 Transfer the mashed potato to a serving dish and top with the remaining onions and bacon. Sprinkle over the paprika and serve.

POTATO GRATIN WITH HAM

SOUTHERN FRANCE

This rustic dish takes modest ingredients — potato slices, onion, ham and two cheeses — and layers and bakes them into something special. A warming welcome for a cold day.

INGREDIENTS
(Serves 4)

- 1kg/2¼lb all-purpose potatoes, e.g. Romano
- salt and black pepper
- butter, for greasing
- 1 onion
- 150g/5oz Gruyère cheese
- 100g/4oz cooked ham
- 2 eggs
- 250ml/9fl oz milk
- pinch of paprika
- 1 tbsp chopped fresh parsley or 1 tsp dried
- 40g/1½oz Sbrinz or Parmesan cheese

INGREDIENTS TIP

Sbrinz is a full-fat cows' milk cheese from Switzerland. It has a dark yellow rind and hard, brittle texture and is very similar to Parmesan. It is almost always used for cooking rather than as a table cheese.

1 Preheat the oven to 180°C/350°F/Gas 4. Wash and peel the potatoes, then cook them in a pan of lightly salted, boiling water for 15–20 minutes, or until almost tender when pierced with a sharp knife.

2 Meanwhile, grease a large, shallow ovenproof dish with butter. Peel and finely chop the onion and sprinkle it into the dish. Coarsely grate the Gruyère and chop the ham.

Step 3

3 Drain the potatoes, leave to cool slightly, then cut into 1cm/½in slices. Layer the potatoes in the dish, overlapping the slices, and sprinkling them with the ham and Gruyère. Finish with a layer of potato on top.

Step 3

4 Beat the eggs with the milk, salt, pepper, paprika and parsley. Pour this mixture slowly over the potatoes. Grate the Sbrinz or Parmesan and sprinkle on top.

5 Bake in the oven for 45 minutes, or until golden brown and crisp. After 30 minutes cover tightly with foil if the potatoes look as if they are browning too quickly. Serve immediately from the dish or spoon individual portions onto serving plates.

Step 4

Preparation **40** Min Cooking **45** Min
Per Serving: 515 kcal/2161 kJ;
29g protein; 21g fat; 55g carbohydrate

TYPICALLY FRENCH

This potato dish is a sophisticated version of Gratin Dauphinois which is made with sliced potatoes, milk and eggs. Gratin Dauphinois originates from the mountainous Dauphiné region where dishes are hearty and make the most of local produce such as cheese and ham.

COOKING TIP

Take care not to overcook the potatoes during the
initial boiling stage, or they will break up when baked
in the oven. Keep the water at a steady, rather than a
fast, boil and test with the tip of a sharp knife. The
potatoes are ready when they feel tender but still offer
a little resistance when pierced.

SERVING TIP

This dish is perfect with
grilled lamb chops and a
tomato and basil salad.

 A light French red wine, such as a Beaujolais,
would go well with this dish.

31

POTATOES WITH SOUFFLE FILLING

SOUTHERN FRANCE

These hollowed-out potato skins are filled with a herby soufflé, then baked until crisp. The irresistible result is a light, fluffy filling in a crunchy golden shell.

INGREDIENTS

(Serves 4)

- 4 large floury potatoes (about 1kg/2¼lb), e.g. Pentland Squire or King Edward
- olive oil, for brushing
- 15g/½oz butter
- 2 eggs, separated
- 2 tsp dried herbes de Provence
- salt and black pepper

INGREDIENTS TIP

Choose potatoes that are roughly equal in size, evenly-shaped and flattish, so that they sit securely in the baking dish after they have been filled.

1 Preheat the oven to 200°C/400°F/Gas 6. Scrub the potatoes under cold running water and cut out any small blemishes with the tip of a sharp knife. Prick each potato several times with a fork and brush with olive oil, then place in the oven.

2 Bake for 1 hour, or until the potatoes are crisp outside and soft inside. Leave until cool enough to handle, then slice off the tops lengthwise and scoop out the flesh with a spoon, taking care not to damage the skins. Place the potato flesh in a bowl.

3 Mash the potato flesh until smooth. Stir in the butter, egg yolks and herbs. Season with salt and pepper.

4 Whisk the egg whites until stiff, then fold them into the potato mixture using a large metal spoon. Pile the mixture back into the skins, gently easing it down into them.

5 Arrange the filled potatoes in an ovenproof dish and return to the oven for about 30 minutes, or until risen, golden brown and crisp on top. Serve immediately.

Step 2

Step 2

Step 4

Preparation **15** Min
Cooking **1** Hour **30** Min
Per Serving: 341 kcal/1446 kJ;
11g protein; 6g fat; 64g carbohydrate

TYPICALLY PROVENCAL

Lavender grows all over Provence and the shimmering purple fields are a popular sight in June and July. The dried flower heads are used to perfume soap and other toiletries. As a herb, lavender is frequently added to the dried mix known as herbes de Provence.

COOKING TIPS

To check whether the potatoes are completely cooked, push a thin metal skewer into the centre of each. The flesh should be so soft that the skewer slides in easily • To speed up cooking, microwave the potatoes on full power for 15 minutes. Transfer to the oven for 20-30 minutes at Step 2 to crisp the skins.

SERVING TIP

A pepper and tomato salad is the ideal accompaniment to turn these potatoes into a tempting light meal.

Serve with a chilled white Côtes de Rhône or a white wine spritzer.

𝒫ATATAS BRAVAS

SPAIN

Bravas means rough or rugged in Spanish. These crispy potato chunks are a popular country dish in Spain where they are served with aïoli, a thick garlic and mayonnaise dip.

INGREDIENTS
(Serves 4)

- 600g/1lb 5oz all-purpose potatoes, e.g. Romano
- salt and white pepper
- 4 cloves garlic
- 175ml/6fl oz good-quality mayonnaise
- 4 tbsp olive oil

INGREDIENTS TIP

Large, oval potatoes are best for cutting into neat cubes as they can first be cut in good-sized slices, then into strips and finally diced. The bigger the potato slices, the fewer curved edges they will have so the cubes will be more evenly shaped.

1 Thoroughly scrub the potatoes, then cook them in lightly salted, boiling water for about 20 minutes, or until tender.

2 To make the garlic and mayonnaise dip, peel the garlic and place in a mortar. Sprinkle with a little salt and crush with a pestle to a fine pulp. If you don't have a pestle and mortar, mash the garlic with a fork in a bowl.

Step 2

3 Gradually mix in the mayonnaise and season with salt and pepper. Cover and leave the flavours to blend.

4 Drain the potatoes and set aside until cool enough to handle. Peel and cut them into 2.5cm/1in chunks.

Step 5

5 Heat the olive oil in a large frying pan. Add the potatoes and fry, turning occasionally with a slotted spoon, until golden brown and crisp on all sides.

6 Drain the fried potatoes on kitchen paper. Season generously and serve with the aïoli in a separate bowl.

Step 6

Preparation **15** Min Cooking **25** Min
Per Serving: 690 kcal/980 kJ;
12g protein; 9g fat; 27g carbohydrate

TYPICALLY SPANISH

Crispy potatoes are one of many Spanish tapas, or little appetizers offered with drinks in bars and at home. Tapa literally means lid in Spanish — bar owners used to put plates of bread, cheese or ham on top of glasses of sherry to preserve the flavour of the drink.

COOKING TIP

Olive oil is excellent for frying as it remains stable at high temperatures. Choose a light gold pure olive oil (a mixture of virgin and refined) as this has a pleasantly mild flavour, rather than a strong-flavoured deep green virgin oil which would be too dominant for this particular dish.

SERVING TIP

For a selection of tapas, serve with pimiento-stuffed olives, fried prawns and marinated peppers.

A dry or medium-dry sherry is traditionally served with this potato dish.

TORTILLA WITH VEGETABLES

Here the classic Spanish tortilla, or potato omelette, is given a twist by adding courgettes and colourful red peppers. The omelette is fried gently for a crisp exterior and creamy centre.

INGREDIENTS
(Serves 4)

- 600g/1lb 5oz all-purpose potatoes, e.g. Maris Piper
- 300g/10½oz courgettes
- 1 red pepper
- 2 large onions
- 6 tbsp olive oil
- 2 cloves garlic
- bunch of fresh parsley
- salt and black pepper
- 6 eggs
- flat-leaved parsley, to garnish

INGREDIENTS TIP

Large Spanish onions are the classic choice for this omelette as their mild flavour does not overpower the pepper and potatoes.

1 Peel, wash and thinly slice the potatoes and courgettes. Wash the pepper, then halve, de-seed and roughly chop it. Peel the onions, cut them in half and slice finely.

2 Heat 3 tablespoons of oil in a large frying pan. Fry the potatoes, pepper and onions over a medium heat for 5 minutes, or until slightly soft, then add the courgettes and fry for 2 minutes, until they are slightly softened and the potatoes cooked through. Peel and crush the garlic, then add to the pan.

3 Wash, dry and finely chop the fresh parsley, discarding the tough stalks. Mix with the vegetables in the pan and season.

4 Beat the eggs. Add the remaining oil to the pan and heat for a few seconds. Pour the eggs over the vegetable mixture. Cover and cook over a low heat for 8 minutes, until the eggs are set, shaking the pan a few times to prevent the omelette from sticking.

5 Slide the omelette onto a plate, turn it upside down onto another plate or board, then slide it back into the pan. Cook for a further 6–8 minutes, until golden. Cut into wedges and garnish. Serve hot or cold.

Step 1

Step 4

Step 5

Preparation **15** Min Cooking **30** Min
Per Serving: 480 kcal/2010 kJ;
15g protein; 35g fat; 26g carbohydrate

TYPICALLY SPANISH

Traditional Tortilla de Patatas consists of only potatoes and eggs, and is basically a simple, rustic omelette. Spaniards owe this dish to the Conquistadors, who left Spain to conquer America in 1518 — and who brought back the humble potato.

COOKING TIP

It is important to cook the potatoes completely
before adding the eggs. Frying them with the red
pepper and onions gives the tortilla its characteristic
flavour. The tortilla is at its best when golden brown
on the outside and still slightly moist inside, with
the eggs only just set.

SERVING TIP

Serve this tortilla as a starter, or
with hunks of white bread and
a green salad for lunch.

A chilled Spanish white wine, such as a Rioja, is
perfect with this traditional dish.

HERBY POTATO FANS

SOUTHERN ITALY

These thinly sliced potatoes, baked with Parmesan, rosemary, thyme and garlic, make a crispy side dish that will fill your kitchen with the appetizing aroma of Mediterranean cooking.

INGREDIENTS
(Serves 4)

- 4 large baking potatoes, e.g. Estima (about 1kg/2¼lb)
- 3 tbsp olive oil
- 2 sprigs fresh rosemary or 2 tsp dried
- 6 sprigs fresh thyme or 2 tsp dried
- 4 cloves garlic
- 6 tbsp fresh white breadcrumbs
- 25g/1oz butter
- salt and black pepper
- 50g/2oz Parmesan cheese
- fresh rosemary, to garnish

INGREDIENTS TIP

It is best to buy a block of Parmesan and grate it when needed. This way its aroma and taste is retained much better than if the cheese is bought pre-grated in a tub.

1 Preheat the oven to 180°C/350°F/Gas 4. Peel the potatoes, then cut them in half lengthways and slice them thinly, holding the slices firmly together. Grease a baking dish with a little of the olive oil.

Step 1

2 Place the potatoes in the dish (see Cooking tip), each in an attractive fan shape. Wash, dry with kitchen paper and finely chop the fresh rosemary and thyme, if using, discarding the stalks.

3 Peel and finely chop the garlic. Mix the chopped fresh or dried herbs and garlic with the breadcrumbs, then sprinkle this mixture evenly over the potato fans.

Step 4

4 Melt the butter in a small saucepan. Add the olive oil, salt and pepper, then spoon evenly over the potatoes, making sure that the liquid seeps in between the slices.

5 Bake for about 40 minutes. Grate the Parmesan and sprinkle it over the potatoes, then bake for a further 15 minutes, until the topping is crisp and golden and the potatoes are tender. Garnish with sprigs of fresh rosemary and serve.

Step 5

Preparation **30** Min Cooking **55** Min
Per Serving: 386 kcal/1619 kJ;
11g protein; 19g fat; 47g carbohydrate

TYPICALLY ITALIAN

In Apulia, a rural area on the south east 'heel' of Italy, grain, potatoes and vegetables are popular items on local menus. These simple ingredients are often combined with garlic-flavoured olive oil and wild fresh herbs to create basic, but tasty, dishes.

COOKING TIP

To ensure the prepared potato fans keep their shape, slide a wide-bladed knife or a metal slice horizontally under each potato half and transfer it carefully to the baking dish before cooking. Hold the knife or slice in one hand and carefully ease the potato slices into the dish with your other hand.

SERVING TIP

Serve as a side dish with breaded chicken, or grilled lamb cutlets, garnished with lemon.

 A white wine, such as San Severo from Apulia, goes well with this dish.

LEMON AND GARLIC POTATOES

GREECE

The evocative aroma of new potatoes fried in olive oil, then simmered in stock and seasoned with lemon and garlic will recreate the atmosphere of fondly remembered Greek holidays.

INGREDIENTS
(Serves 4)

- 800g/1¾lb waxy potatoes, e.g. Jersey Royal
- 5 cloves garlic
- 4 tbsp olive oil
- 250ml/9fl oz hot vegetable stock
- salt and black pepper
- 1 lemon
- 1 tbsp fresh thyme or 1 tsp dried
- 1 tbsp fresh rosemary or 1 tsp dried
- chopped fresh thyme and rosemary, to garnish

INGREDIENTS TIP

Buy small potatoes of roughly equal size so that they cook evenly throughout.

1 Scrub the potatoes under cold running water, then dry them on kitchen paper. Peel and thinly slice the garlic.

2 Heat the oil in a large, heavy-based frying pan. Gently fry the garlic until golden, then remove with a slotted spoon. Place on kitchen paper to drain.

Step 2

3 Briefly fry and turn the potatoes in the oil remaining in the pan. Pour in the stock, season with salt and pepper, then bring to the boil. Reduce the heat, cover and simmer for 25 minutes, or until the potatoes are tender, but still firm, when pierced with the point of a sharp knife.

Step 4

4 Wash the lemon under hot running water, then pat it dry. Finely grate the rind and squeeze out the juice. Wash and dry the fresh thyme and rosemary, if using. Chop the leaves and discard the stems.

5 Add the lemon juice and rind, thyme and rosemary to the potatoes. Cook uncovered for 5 minutes over a high heat, until the stock has reduced. Sprinkle with the garlic and serve.

Step 5

Preparation **20** Min Cooking **30** Min
Per Serving: 283 kcal/1184 kJ;
4g protein; 16g fat; 33g carbohydrate

TYPICALLY GREEK
The Greeks were creating wonderful dishes 500 years before the birth of Christ. The Greek Hasiod is credited with writing one of the world's first cook books. Today, their delicious, simple dishes, made with local produce are still renowned worldwide.

Cooking tip
The potatoes are simmered in the stock rather than cooked on a fast boil, so they absorb more of its flavour. Keep the lid on the pan so the liquid does not evaporate and the pan boil dry. A home-made or fresh shop-bought stock will give a better, less salty flavour than stock cubes.

Serving tip

For a simple lunch, sprinkle cubed feta over the potatoes, and serve with marinated peppers.

 Try a Greek red wine such as a Nemea from the Peloponnese, or a French Fitou.

SERVING TIP Serve as a starter or as an accompaniment to roast lamb.

Choose a full-bodied red wine, such as Shiraz or Zinfandel, to serve with this dish.

𝒫OTATOES WITH AUBERGINE

TURKEY

Crisp, golden potatoes and succulent pieces of aubergine are flavoured with chillies and paprika in this Turkish recipe. A chilled yoghurt sauce provides the perfect cooling dip.

INGREDIENTS

(Serves 4)

- 500g/1lb 2oz waxy potatoes, e.g. Cara
- 6 tbsp olive oil
- salt and black pepper
- 1 aubergine
- 3–4 large green chillies
- ½ tsp paprika
- flat-leaved parsley or mint sprigs, to garnish

FOR THE SAUCE

- 2 tbsp chopped fresh parsley
- 1 tbsp chopped fresh mint
- 300ml/½ pint Greek-style yoghurt

INGREDIENTS TIP

Creamy Greek-style yoghurt has a rich flavour. You can also use full-fat natural yoghurt, although it will make the sauce less creamy. As a general rule, the thinner the chilli, the hotter it is.

1 Peel the potatoes and cut into 2.5cm/1in chunks. Heat the olive oil in a large frying pan. Add the potatoes, season with salt and pepper, then fry over a medium heat for about 10 minutes, turning regularly with a wooden spatula to ensure that all sides are golden and crisp.

Step 1

2 Meanwhile, wash the aubergine, trim the stalk end and cut the flesh into 1cm/½in dice. Wearing rubber gloves, cut the stalks off the chillies, slice open and remove the seeds. Cut the chillies into fine strips.

3 Add the aubergine and chilli to the frying pan. Stir in the paprika and fry for another 15 minutes, turning regularly.

Step 3

4 For the sauce, whisk the chopped fresh parsley and mint into the yoghurt. Season with salt and pepper to taste.

5 When the potatoes and aubergines are tender, transfer the vegetables to a warm serving dish and garnish with the sprigs of parsley or mint. Serve the yoghurt sauce separately in a small bowl.

Step 4

Preparation **15** Min Cooking **25** Min
Per Serving: 270 kcal/1150 kJ;
5g protein; 19g fat; 21g carbohydrate

TYPICALLY TURKISH

For many centuries, since the times when the majority of the population was nomadic, traditional Turkish cuisine has made extensive use of yoghurt. Many country households produce their own refreshing yoghurt from ewes', cows' or goats' milk.

ISRAELI VEGETABLE KEBABS

Treat your guests to these delightful potato, onion, pepper and courgette kebabs, well-seasoned with aromatic herbs and spices and grilled to crisp perfection.

INGREDIENTS
(Serves 4)

- 400g/14oz waxy potatoes, e.g. Jersey Royal
- 1 small onion
- 2 small courgettes
- 1 red pepper
- 8 bay leaves
- 1 tbsp chopped fresh thyme or 1 tsp dried
- 6 tbsp olive oil
- salt and black pepper
- ¼ tsp caraway seeds
- ¼ tsp ground allspice
- ¼ tsp ground cinnamon
- ¼ tsp ground cardamom
- fresh thyme and flat-leaved parsley, to garnish

INGREDIENTS TIP

As Jersey Royal have only a short season of around two months each year, substitute other small new potatoes when not available.

1 Peel the potatoes, then cut them into 1cm/½in thick slices. Cook in lightly salted, boiling water for just under 10 minutes, then drain in a colander.

2 Peel and halve the onion, then carefully separate the individual layers. Put the onions into salted boiling water and cook for 1 minute, then drain. Cut the courgettes into 1–2cm/½–¾in thick slices. Halve and de-seed the pepper, and cut it into pieces, roughly the same size as the other vegetables.

Step 2

3 Carefully thread the vegetables onto four metal or wooden skewers, alternating the pieces of potato, onion, courgette and pepper. Add 2 bay leaves per skewer for flavour, but remove before eating.

Step 3

4 Mix the thyme with the olive oil, salt, pepper, caraway seeds, allspice, cinnamon and cardamom. Heat the grill to high.

5 Brush the kebabs with the oil mixture and grill for about 10 minutes, until golden on all sides, turning the skewers and brushing the vegetables several times with the oil to prevent them drying out. Garnish with thyme and parsley and serve immediately.

Step 5

Preparation **15** Min Cooking **20** Min
Per Serving: 322 kcal/1339 kJ;
3g protein; 23g fat; 28g carbohydrate

TYPICALLY ISRAELI

In Israel, marinated and heavily spiced meat kebabs are on offer at virtually every restaurant, food stall on the streets and at every barbecue. Many small, open-fronted restaurants also offer ready-prepared meat and vegetable dishes to passers-by.

COOKING TIPS

The potatoes have to be partly boiled, as they will not
be made tender by grilling alone. However, do not
overcook them or they will fall apart when threaded
onto the skewers • The kebabs are ideal for outdoor
barbecues. Use metal skewers and watch them
carefully as they can easily overcook over hot charcoal.

SERVING TIP

Serve with a tomato sauce as an
accompaniment to grilled or fried
fish or chicken.

 A cool glass of iced mineral water with a dash of
lime cordial would go well with the kebabs.

$\mathscr{S}$PICY POTATO CURRY

INDIA

Potatoes are excellent in curries as their starchy texture perfectly balances the spicy ingredients. Here, whole spices give this aromatic dish a superb flavour and slight crunch.

INGREDIENTS
(Serves 4)

- 1kg/2¼lb waxy potatoes, e.g. Pink Fir Apple
- 2 large onions
- 2.5cm/1in piece root ginger
- 1 clove garlic
- 2 tbsp coriander seeds
- 4 green cardamom pods
- 50g/2oz ghee or vegetable oil
- 1 tbsp mustard seeds
- 1 tbsp cumin seeds
- 1 cinnamon stick
- 1 bay leaf
- 1 tsp turmeric
- salt and black pepper
- 300ml/½ pint vegetable stock
- 75g/3oz frozen peas
- coriander leaves, to garnish

INGREDIENTS TIP

Select fresh ginger that is plump, pale and fairly thin-skinned. Avoid shrivelled or thick-skinned, woody roots.

1 Wash and scrub the potatoes. Peel and thinly slice the onions. Peel and chop the ginger and garlic. Finely crush the coriander seeds with a pestle in a mortar. Split the cardamom pods, scrape out the seeds and add them to the coriander.

Step 1

2 Heat half the ghee or vegetable oil in a frying pan. Add the coriander mixture, mustard and cumin seeds, cinnamon stick and bay leaf. Fry the spices over a medium heat for 2 minutes, or until they begin to sizzle and pop slightly.

3 Add half the onions, the ginger, garlic and potatoes. Cook, stirring, until the onions are tender. Stir in the turmeric, salt and pepper. Transfer to a shallow, flame-proof casserole dish. Add the stock and peas and bring to the boil. Reduce the heat, cover and simmer for 10 minutes. Meanwhile, fry the remaining onions in the remaining ghee or vegetable oil until golden. Set aside.

Step 3

4 Remove the casserole lid, stir and cook for a further 10 minutes, until most of the liquid has evaporated and the potatoes are tender. Garnish with the coriander leaves and serve with the onions on the side.

Step 3

Preparation **20** Min Cooking **25** Min
Per Serving: 289 kcal/1212 kJ; 8g protein; 10g fat; 44g carbohydrate

TYPICALLY INDIAN

Ghee, or clarified butter, is used in many traditional Indian dishes. Nowadays, however, vegetable fat is used as an alternative. For some dishes, particularly dhal (lentils cooked with spices), whole spices are fried in ghee and poured over the cooked dish.

SERVING TIP Serve with tandoori chicken or fish; or with dhal or egg curry for a vegetarian meal.

 Try a chilled beer, or a natural yoghurt and fruit juice drink with this dish.

SERVING TIP Offer a fruit chutney, such as peach, mango or tomato, with these savoury spirals.

 Try Indian tea flavoured with a cinnamon stick or cloves with this spicy dish.

SAVOURY POTATO AND COCONUT SPIRALS

INDIA

Serve these spirals as a delicious snack or a tasty side dish. The spicy mash is rolled up in a wafer-thin pastry, then sliced and fried until golden brown.

INGREDIENTS
(Serves 4)

- 600g/1lb 5oz floury potatoes, e.g. King Edward
- salt and pepper
- 2 red chillies
- 4cm/1½in piece root ginger or 2 tsp ground
- 4 tbsp desiccated coconut
- 1 tsp sesame seeds
- 1 tsp brown sugar
- 2 tsp garam masala

FOR THE PASTRY

- 1 tbsp ghee or butter, plus extra for frying
- 200g/7oz plain flour, plus extra for dusting
- 1 tbsp turmeric
- 1 tbsp vegetable oil, for frying

INGREDIENTS TIP

Ghee is available from some large supermarkets or Asian shops as 'concentrated butter for cooking and baking'.

1 Scrub the potatoes, then cook them in a pan of lightly salted, boiling water for 20 minutes, or until tender. Drain, leave until cool enough to handle, then peel and mash.

2 Wearing rubber gloves, wash and halve the chillies, de-seed, then finely chop. Peel and finely chop the root ginger. Mix the chillies and ginger with the desiccated coconut, sesame seeds, sugar and garam masala. Mix in the potatoes and salt and pepper to taste. Leave the mixture to cool.

3 To make the pastry, melt the ghee or butter in a pan. Sift the flour into a bowl, then add the fat, turmeric and 125ml/4fl oz cold water. Press together into a dough.

4 On a lightly floured surface, roll out the dough to about 40x25cm/16x10in. Spread with the potato mixture, leaving a border around the edge. Roll up the dough and filling. Cut into 2cm/¾in slices.

5 Heat plenty of ghee or butter with the oil in a large frying pan. Fry the spirals in batches for 5 minutes on each side, until golden and sizzling. Remove with a spatula and drain on kitchen paper. Serve warm.

Step 3

Step 4

Step 4

Preparation **20** Min Cooking **50** Min
Per Serving: 498 kcal/3000 kJ;
10g protein; 16g fat; 83g carbohydrate

TYPICALLY BENGALI

The vast metropolis of Calcutta, in West Bengal, was the capital of the British Raj until 1912. Its cuisine is influenced by Hindus, Muslims, Jews and Christians providing a scintillating hotch-potch of sweet and savoury dishes.

3 WAYS WITH BAKED POTATOES

Baked potatoes were originally served as side dishes with meat, but now, served with delicious toppings they are meals in their own right.

BASIC BAKED POTATOES

Preparation **5** Min   Cooking **1** Hour

(SERVES 4)
- 4 floury potatoes, e.g. Golden Wonder or King Edward
- 1 tbsp vegetable oil
- salt and black pepper

1 Preheat the oven to 200°C/400°F/Gas 6. Scrub the potatoes, cut out any blemishes, then pat dry on kitchen paper. Prick with a fork, brush with vegetable oil and sprinkle with salt and pepper.

2 Put on a baking tray. Bake for 1 hour, or until the skins are crisp and the centres are soft when pierced with a knife. Wrap in foil before baking if you prefer the skins to be soft.

MOZZARELLA AND HERB POTATOES

Preparation **10** Min   Cooking **5** Min

ITALY

(SERVES 4)
- 4 baked potatoes
- 2 tbsp pine nuts
- 125g/4½oz mozzarella cheese
- 2 small tomatoes
- 1 clove garlic
- 2 tbsp chopped fresh basil
- 2 tbsp chopped fresh parsley
- salt and black pepper

3 Roast the pine nuts in a dry frying pan over a low heat until lightly browned. Dice the mozzarella. Wash, de-seed and finely chop the tomatoes. Peel and crush the garlic. Mix these ingredients with the herbs and season.

4 Cut a cross in the top of each potato, then gently squeeze open. Fill with the herb mixture and grill for 5 minutes until hot.

MEXICAN BEAN POTATOES

Preparation **15** Min Cooking **10** Min

(SERVES 4)

- 4 baked potatoes
- 1 onion
- 1 clove garlic
- 2 green chillies
- 2 tbsp sunflower oil
- 400g/14oz can red kidney beans
- 225g/8oz can chopped tomatoes
- salt and black pepper
- 1 small avocado
- 3 tbsp lemon juice

4 Drain the kidney beans and rinse in a sieve, then add to the onion mixture with the tomatoes, salt and pepper. Simmer over a low heat for 10 minutes, stirring occasionally.

5 Halve the avocado and discard the stone, then peel and dice the flesh. Sprinkle with lemon juice.

6 Cut a cross in the top of each potato and gently squeeze open. Stir together the bean mixture and the avocado, then spoon into the potatoes. Serve immediately.

3 Peel and finely chop the onion and garlic. Wash, de-seed and chop the chillies. Heat the oil in a pan and fry onion, garlic and chillies for 3 minutes until golden.

CREAMY BROCCOLI POTATOES

Preparation **15** Min Cooking **5** Min

(SERVES 4)

- 4 baked potatoes
- 200g/7oz broccoli
- salt and black pepper
- 200ml/7fl oz crème fraîche
- 2 tbsp chopped fresh parsley
- 100g/4oz Cheddar or Gouda cheese
- 4 tsp butter

3 Wash and trim the broccoli. Cut into florets. Cook in lightly salted, boiling water for 5 minutes, then drain.

4 Mix the crème fraîche with the parsley, salt and pepper. Grate the cheese.

5 Cut a cross in the top of each potato and gently squeeze open. Add 1 tsp of butter and a little of the grated cheese to each.

6 Mix the broccoli and crème fraîche, then spoon it into the potatoes. Sprinkle the remaining cheese on top of each potato and grill for 5 minutes to heat through.

POTATO AND HAM PATTIES

These succulent potato patties are flavoured with a little ham and cheese. Pepped up with chilli sauce and served in a bun, they make a delicious alternative to the traditional beefburger.

INGREDIENTS

(Serves 4)

- 350g/12oz floury potatoes, e.g. Pentland Squire
- 50g/2oz cooked ham
- 50g/2oz Emmental cheese
- 7g/¼oz butter
- 2 tbsp chopped fresh parsley or 1 tsp dried
- salt and black pepper
- flour, for dusting
- 4 tbsp dried white breadcrumbs
- 4 tbsp sunflower oil, for frying
- 4 round bread rolls
- bunch of fresh watercress
- 125g/4½oz crème fraîche
- 3 tbsp chilli sauce

INGREDIENTS TIP

Buy good-quality cooked ham, such as one carved off the bone or a honey-roast ham, to give these patties plenty of flavour.

1 Preheat the oven to 200°C/400°F/Gas 6. Scrub the potatoes, put on a baking tray and cook for 1 hour, or until the skins are crisp and the flesh is soft. Leave until cool enough to handle, then halve the potatoes and scoop out the flesh into a bowl and mash with a fork.

Step 1

2 Dice the ham and Emmental cheese. Melt the butter and stir into the potato with the ham, cheese and parsley. Season with salt and pepper.

3 Divide the mixture into quarters. Dust your hands with flour and shape each portion into a flat patty, pressing the mixture together firmly. Press into the breadcrumbs to coat and chill in the fridge for 1 hour.

Step 2

4 Heat the oil in a frying pan and fry the patties for 10 minutes, turning carefully once, until golden brown. Keep warm.

5 Slice the rolls in half and toast the cut sides. Wash the watercress. Mix the crème fraîche with the chilli sauce, then spread on each roll, place watercress leaves and a patty on top. Cover with the remaining chilli cream and the top of the roll. Garnish with watercress.

Step 3

Preparation 15 Min Chilling 1 Hour
Cooking 1 Hour 10 Min
Per Serving: 495 kcal/2065 kJ;
14g protein; 32g fat; 41g carbohydrate

TYPICALLY AUSTRALIAN

British immigrants introduced watercress to Australia, establishing the characteristic water beds essential for commercial farming. It is used as a tangy garnish for barbecued dishes such as traditional hamburgers and barbecued fish and prawns.

COOKING TIP

When baking or boiling potatoes, cook a few extra and make these into patties, on a tray covered with cling film. Open-freeze when firm, then pack in a polythene bag and freeze for up to 3 months. Cook from frozen, allowing a little extra time for the mixture to thaw and heat through.

SERVING TIP

Offer various ready-made sauces, such as tomato ketchup, mayonnaise or Tabasco sauce to enhance the flavour of the patties.

 An ice-cold beer is the traditional Australian accompaniment to summer food.

CALIFORNIAN CRISPY POTATO WEDGES

USA

Hot, crispy roasted potato wedges are flavoured with dried herbs and a hint of spice. Serve with a cool, tangy dip of fresh herbs and sour cream.

INGREDIENTS
(Serves 4)

- 6 large waxy potatoes, e.g. Estima or Cara
- 2 tbsp vegetable oil
- salt and black pepper
- ½ tsp ground mace
- 1 tsp dried thyme
- 300ml/½ pint sour cream
- 2 tbsp chopped fresh parsley
- 1tbsp chopped fresh dill or 1 tsp dried
- 1 tbsp chopped fresh tarragon or 1 tsp dried
- grated rind of ½ lemon

INGREDIENTS TIP

Since it is only the skin that is used for this dish, there is no need to be too fussy about the precise choice of potatoes. Choose main crop potatoes as they have thick skins, and not the fine-skinned new potatoes.

1 Preheat the oven to 200°C/400°F/Gas 6. Scrub the potatoes. Use the point of a knife to cut out any blemishes in the skin, then cut each potato into quarters lengthways.

2 Hold a piece of potato skin-side down. Using a small pointed knife carefully cut as far as the middle of the wedge, following the line of the skin and about 6mm/¼in inside it. Turn the potato and do the same on the other side. This will free a piece of potato and leave you with a curved skin.

3 Repeat with the remaining potato pieces, then put the wedges in a polythene bag. (Save the leftover potato for another recipe.) Add the oil, a good sprinkling of salt, the mace and thyme to the wedges. Hold the bag closed and shake it gently to coat the potatoes with the oil and flavourings.

4 Arrange the wedges on a baking sheet, skin side up, and bake in the oven for about 50 minutes, or until crisp and golden. Meanwhile, mix the sour cream, parsley, dill, tarragon, lemon rind and a little salt and pepper. Chill. Serve the hot wedges with the cold herb and soured cream dip.

Step 1

Step 3

Step 4

Preparation **15** Min Cooking **50** Min
Per Serving: 766 kcal/3210 kJ;
12g protein; 44g fat; 87g carbohydrate

TYPICALLY CALIFORNIAN

West coast American restaurants have a casual eating style where easy-to-eat snack food such as sandwiches, burgers, fries and muffins are popular. San Francisco, on the Californian coast, has a host of ocean-side eateries around its shoreline and local beaches.

COOKING TIP

The potato skins can also be fried, if you prefer. Heat oil for deep-frying to 190°C/375°F, or until hot enough to brown a cube of bread in 30 seconds. Place the skins in a frying basket. Plunge into the hot oil and deep-fry for 2–3 minutes, or until golden brown and crisp. Drain on kitchen paper.

SERVING TIP

Serve with crunchy fresh vegetables such as cucumber and carrot sticks and a crisp green salad.

 Potato wedges are great with sparkling soft drinks, fruit juice or flavoured mineral water.

SERVING TIP Serve with chargrilled steaks, topped with a herb butter.

 Ice-cold beer or pale dry cider is perfect with these sweet potatoes.

SWEET POTATO FRITTERS

CARIBBEAN

Bright orange slices of sweet potato are dusted with a spicy coating and fried until crisp and golden. Serve with a squeeze of fresh lime for that unmistakable Caribbean taste.

INGREDIENTS

(Serves 4)

- 700g/1½lb sweet potatoes
- salt and black pepper
- 1 clove garlic
- 6 tbsp plain flour
- ½ tsp ground cinnamon
- ½ tsp grated nutmeg
- ¼ tsp cayenne pepper
- 25g/1oz butter
- 2 tbsp groundnut oil
- 3 tbsp chopped fresh parsley, to garnish
- 2 limes, to serve

INGREDIENTS TIP

Freshly grated nutmeg has a far better flavour than pre-ground. Whole nutmegs are sold in jars in the spice section of most supermarkets. A special fine, but tough, grater is useful, so you can grate the spice as you need it.

1 Peel and wash the potatoes, then cut into fairly thick slices. Put in lightly salted, boiling water for about 5 minutes, then plunge into cold water. Drain and leave until cool enough to handle.

2 Peel and finely chop the garlic, then put in a shallow dish or on a plate. Add the flour, cinnamon, nutmeg and cayenne pepper. Season generously with salt and a little black pepper. Mix well.

3 Melt the butter with the oil in a large frying pan. Dip a few of the sweet potato slices into the seasoned flour, turning them to coat all sides, then add to the pan.

4 Cook over a medium heat for about 5 minutes on each side, until golden brown and tender when pierced in the centre with the point of a knife. Drain on kitchen paper and keep hot while coating and cooking the remaining slices.

5 Arrange the sweet potato fritters on a plate and sprinkle with the parsley. Cut the limes into wedges and serve with the fritters, so that the juice may be squeezed over just before eating.

Step 1

Step 3

Step 4

Preparation **20** Min Cooking **35** Min
Per Serving: 397 kcal/1675 kJ;
5g protein; 14g fat; 68g carbohydrate

TYPICALLY CARIBBEAN

Sweet potatoes are native to central America and the Caribbean islands and are sold in markets alongside other vegetables that flourish in the sun. Other popular West Indian vegetables are plantains (cooking bananas) and cassavas which are ground and used as a nutty seasoning.

SPECIAL POTATO CAKES

These golden potato cakes, or 'Llapingachos' as they are known in Ecuador, are traditionally sprinkled with cinnamon. Try them with or without the spice, as a tasty snack or side dish.

INGREDIENTS
(Serves 4)

- 750g/1lb 10oz floury potatoes, e.g. King Edward
- salt and black pepper
- 2 onions
- 15g/½oz butter
- 2 small eggs
- 100g/4oz Gouda cheese
- plain flour, for coating
- 2 tbsp vegetable oil
- ¼ tsp turmeric
- ground cinnamon, to serve (optional)

INGREDIENTS TIP

The oil used to fry these potato cakes was traditionally coloured with yellowish-red annatto seeds. Turmeric is a good substitute and gives the cakes a wonderful golden hue.

1 Peel and chop the potatoes. Cook in lightly salted, boiling water for about 20 minutes, or until tender.

2 Meanwhile, peel and finely chop the onions. Melt the butter in a pan and gently fry the onions for 5 minutes until soft.

Step 2

3 Drain and mash the potatoes, in the pan but off the heat. Lightly beat the eggs. Add the eggs and onions to the potatoes. Season with plenty of salt and pepper and mix well. Transfer the mixture to a bowl; allow to cool. Cover and chill for 1 hour.

Step 4

4 Divide the potato mixture into 12 portions. Dust your hands with flour. Mould each potato portion into a patty. Slice the cheese into 12 pieces to fit inside the patties. Push a piece of cheese into the centre of each patty and remould. Coat the patties with flour.

5 Heat the oil in a frying pan and stir in the turmeric. Fry the patties in batches, over a medium heat, for 3 minutes on each side, or until golden brown. Remove with a fish slice; drain on kitchen paper and keep warm while cooking the rest. Serve with ground cinnamon, if using.

Step 5

Preparation **20** Min Chilling **1** Hour
Cooking **40** Min
Per Serving: 478 kcal/1995 kJ;
154g protein; 29g fat; 44g carbohydrate

TYPICALLY ECUADORIAN

Many Ecuadorians make a living from selling snacks in markets, on buses and trains, or at the side of roads. These potato cakes are to be found everywhere, especially in the northern part of the Andes and in the capital city of Ecuador, Quito.

COOKING TIP

Chilling the potato mixture at the end of Step 3 is essential as it makes it easier to shape into patties and prevents the cakes disintegrating when they are fried. Let the mixture cool before covering and putting it in the fridge. Chill it for at least 1 hour or for up to 2 hours — the longer the better.

SERVING TIP

Serve with a tomato, avocado and lettuce salad for a snack meal, or as an accompaniment to grilled chicken.

 A chilled glass of tomato juice with a dash of Worcestershire sauce goes well with this dish.

SAUTEED POTATOES WITH PEPPERS

MEXICO

INGREDIENTS
(Serves 4)

- 600g/1lb 5oz new potatoes, e.g. Epicure
- 3 tbsp sunflower oil
- 1 red pepper
- 1 green pepper
- 3-5 small hot chillies
- 2 red onions
- 200g/7oz tomatoes
- salt and black pepper
- 1-2 tbsp lime juice
- chopped fresh coriander, to garnish

INGREDIENTS TIP

Coriander leaves look quite similar to those of flat-leaved parsley but they can be told apart as coriander is sold with its root on. Parsley is always cut cleanly at the root when harvested.

Sweet red peppers, spicy chillies, fresh ripe tomatoes and a hint of lime transform familiar sautéed potatoes into an authentic Mexican dish.

1 Cut the potatoes into 6mm/¼in slices. Heat the oil in a large frying pan. Add the potatoes and fry over a medium heat for about 10 minutes, carefully turning them occasionally, until golden brown and crisp.

2 Meanwhile, wash and remove the seeds from the red and green peppers, then dice finely. Wearing rubber gloves, wash, de-seed and roughly chop the chillies. Peel and finely chop the onions.

3 Add the peppers, onions and chillies to the potatoes and fry for a further 10 minutes, turning the vegetables over frequently to prevent them from sticking.

4 Slit the tomato skins with a sharp knife. Place the tomatoes in a bowl and pour in boiling water to cover. Leave for 1 minute, drain and remove the skins. Quarter the tomatoes, remove and discard the seeds and the core, then dice the flesh.

5 Add the tomatoes to the potatoes and cook for 2 minutes until piping hot. Add salt, pepper and the lime juice. Garnish with chopped coriander and serve immediately.

Step 1

Step 2

Step 4

Preparation **25** Min Cooking **25** Min
Per Serving: 234 kcal/977 kJ;
4g protein; 12g fat; 30g carbohydrate

TYPICALLY MEXICAN
More than 100 varieties of peppers and chillies – from sweet and mild to exceedingly hot – are sold in Mexican markets and used extensively in regional dishes. Years ago Mexicans would rub chillies on their foreheads as a headache cure.

COOKING TIP

The term sauté comes from the French word for jump and in cooking means to fry ingredients over a high heat, turning frequently. Sautéed sliced potatoes should be cooked in a large frying pan so that they brown on both sides; if necessary use two smaller pans instead or fry the slices in batches.

SERVING TIP

This dish makes a perfect side dish for grilled chicken or fried spicy Mexican sausages called chorizillos.

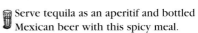 Serve tequila as an aperitif and bottled Mexican beer with this spicy meal.

ᗪICTIONARY OF TERMS

*Master the art of making perfect mash, and add dozens of
other appetizing potato dishes to your repertoire. Introduce
extra flavour with fresh herbs, spices and creamy toppings.*

Aïoli is Mediterranean mayonnaise
made with garlic, egg yolks and
seasoning. Puréed potatoes can be
added for a thicker consistency.

Au gratin is the cooking term
used to describe a dish that is
browned in the oven or under
the grill. Potato gratins are often
made with cheese or eggs.

Baked potatoes can be a meal in
themselves. Rub the skins with a
little olive oil and salt for extra

crispness, then prick
with a fork before
baking. Serve with
cheese and butter
or any of your
other favourite
toppings.

Chips are always popular. For a
perfect result, dry the potato
pieces and cook in oil twice —
once to cook and then, on a
higher heat, to turn golden. Never
cover the deep-fat fryer or pan
with a lid when cooking chips.

Croquettes are mashed potato
shaped into balls or cylinders,
then coated with egg and
breadcrumbs and deep-fried in
hot oil until crisp and golden.

Dauphinois potatoes are very
thinly sliced and layered with
single cream and crushed garlic in
an ovenproof dish. They are then
baked in a low oven until the
creamy flavours are absorbed.

Duchesse potatoes are boiled
potatoes puréed with butter and
egg yolks, then piped into
decorative shapes which are
baked in the oven, or fried, until
crisp and golden on the outside
and fluffy in the middle.

Gnocchi are little Italian
dumplings made from potato
purée, eggs and flour. They are
simmered in plenty of salted
water to cook them, then served
with a tomato or creamy cheese
sauce. They can also be made
with spinach or cheese instead
of the potato purée.

UTENSILS FOR POTATO COOKING

There are plenty of special
cooking utensils to help you get
the best results with different
potato dishes.

PEELER
*A curved blade helps you to strip
away the skin from potatoes. Use
the tip of the peeler to remove
'eyes' or shoots. Swivel peelers
are suitable for left- or
right-handed users.*

ELECTRIC HAND-HELD WHISK
*Put boiled potatoes in a
bowl, then break them up
with a fork. Whisk,
gradually adding milk
and butter until the mash*
*is smooth. Some whisks can be
used directly in a pan, but take
care not to damage the surface.*

POTATO MASHER
*Choose a stainless steel masher,
more effective than plastic, for
an easy, quick way to produce
fluffy mashed potatoes.*

GRATER
*Helpful for finely or roughly
grating potatoes. Many graters
also have a slicer.*

SCRUBBING BRUSH
*A small one is
essential for
cleaning any
dirt from the
skins of new
potatoes and
baking potatoes.*

POTATO TOPPINGS

Add a tasty finishing touch with these easy topping ideas.

SOUR CREAM WITH CHIVES
Mix sour cream with snipped chives and dollop onto fluffy baked potatoes.

HERB BUTTER
Beat chopped fresh parsley, basil and rosemary into softened butter. Spoon onto greaseproof paper and roll into a log shape. Chill until firm; add to mash.

FRIED ONION SHREDS
Gently shallow-fry sliced onions in hot oil until soft, then turn up the heat and cook until golden. Scatter over mashed potatoes.

If you want to perk up any potato dish, just add a few herbs or spices — even the smallest amounts can make a difference.

CHIVES
These are the mildest member of the onion family. Use to flavour mashed potatoes and potato salads.

FIVE-SPICE POWDER
This Chinese mixture of spices has a mild liquorice flavour. Use sparingly or the flavour will be overpowering.

GARAM MASALA
Use this ground spice mixture to pep up fried potatoes or spice up a salad.

MINT
This herb is excellent with new potatoes. Add a few sprigs of fresh mint to the water when you are boiling them.

NUTMEG
A pinch of nutmeg adds a warm flavour to sliced potatoes that are baked in a cream or cheese sauce.

PARSLEY
Chopped parsley adds colour and flavour to mashed potatoes and potato salads.

Mashed potatoes are made by cooking peeled, chopped potatoes in salted, boiling water until tender. Add butter and milk, then mash to a creamy, smooth consistency with a fork or potato masher.

Parboil potatoes that need cooking for a long time to speed up the process. Cook them in boiling water for 5 minutes first to soften slightly. This method is good for roast and sautéed potatoes.

Roast potatoes should be crispy on the outside with a soft, fluffy centre. For best results, cut warm, parboiled potatoes into wedges and drizzle with olive oil. Roast in the oven at 180°C/350°F/ Gas 4 for 45 minutes then turn up the oven to 200°C/400°F/ Gas 6 and cook for 15 minutes, or until crisp and golden.

Rösti is a potato cake or patty made from grated or sliced potatoes. Potatoes are boiled in their jackets until almost done and allowed to cool. Then they are roughly grated and shallow fried in a thick layer in hot fat.

Sautéed potatoes are sliced or diced potatoes fried in butter or oil until crisp and golden. Keep stirring the potatoes to brown them evenly and stop them sticking to the pan.

Tortilla is a Spanish potato omelette. Eggs are poured over parboiled, sliced potatoes in a frying-pan, then cooked over a low heat until the eggs set. The tortilla is then carefully removed from the pan, turned over using two plates, and fried upside down. It can be served hot or cold, cut into slices.

INDEX

Acknowledgements

Picture Credits
All cover and recipe pictures:
Meister Verlag/International Masters Publisher B.V.
Food Photography Karl Adamson, Eising, Dorothee Gödert, Neil Mersh, Peter Rees, Tony Robins, Manuel Schnell, Phillip Wilkins
Agency pictures:
Pictures for the Typically Sections: Agrar Service: Cattlin, Page 52; AKG: Page 36; Anthony Blake: Pages 14, 22; Bavaria: Adam, Page 19; Bav, Page 49; Images, Page 46; Schwarzbach, Page 34; Aberham, Page 43; Diaf, Page 30; Heinzhoch, Page 44; Nägele, Page 32; Rölle, Page 58; Fotex: Arndt, Page 13; Helga Lade: Binder, Page 16; Else, Page 20; Look: Acquadro, Page 10; Robert Harding: Dennis, Page 61; Harris Page 54; Page 57; Schapowalow: Atlantide, Pages 26, 38; Silvestris: Rainer, Page 40; Schneider & Will, Page 8; Stock Market: Page 24

Measuring Ingredients
Tsp – teaspoon, Tbsp – tablespoon
Teaspoons and tablespoons are level and measured using standard measuring spoons.
Follow either metric or imperial measurements and don't mix the two.

© International Masters Publishers BV/
International Masters Publishers Ltd MCMXCVIII
Reproduced by Studio One Origination London, UK
Printed in Verona, Italy, by Druck Mondadori